The Me I See
Answering Life's Questions

* * *

by
The Wood 'N' Barnes Publishing Staff

Acknowledgments

This book was made possible by the generous & creative contributions of:
Chris, Dave, Duane, Gladys, Kacie, James, Jean, Joshua, Mary, Matt, Mony, & Peggy

Thank You All!

Published by:

1st Edition © 1998, Wood 'N' Barnes Publishing., U.S.A.
All rights reserved.

Based on original manuscript by Warren Wiard.
Cover art by Blu Phillips
Copyediting & Design by Ramona Cunningham

Printed in the United States of America
Oklahoma City, Oklahoma
ISBN # 1-885473-20-6

To order copies of this book, please call:
Jean Barnes Books
800-678-0621

INTRODUCTION

by Chris Cavert,
author of Games (& other stuff) for Group, Books 1 & 2,
Affordable Portables, & EAGER Curriculum

Welcome to the adventure. It could be yours, a family member's, or even someone you work with. In any case, this adventure is filled with all the good stuff – challenges and risks, joy and sadness, excitement and fear. All that makes the journey worth the effort, and this journey is a book of questions. These questions lead to a script that has yet to be written. And this script is up to you or anyone willing to travel down the roads of the past, present and future.

Did you know that most of the information on our history has come from books just like this one – journals, if you will? These journals filled with the adventures of explorers, presidents, pioneers, and even children have opened the windows and doors to the lives and times of people just like us. As we read these histories we find the common threads that hold us all together.

What adventures will fill these pages? Pages that lead into yesterday, today and tomorrow. Pages that guide us inside and outside of ourselves. Every turn will provide new opportunities to help discover the adventure yet to be told by you.

Everyone has a story. These stories are all filled with their own peaks and valleys. But these highs and lows are the adventures. All the stories that lead us to where we are and the paths we might choose to risk in the future is the journey. Don't wait. Bring it all to life in these pages of, "The Me I See: Answering Life's Questions."

For the Professional

In order to keep things interesting and to increase the therapeutic value of "The Me I See", we chose to place the questions randomly. We realize there are times when the educator, counselor, therapist or facilitator may want to focus on a particular subject. To make this easier we have provided the following list of topics along with the numbers of the questions that fit that particular topic.

PAST
(personal history/prior experience)

12, 14, 20, 27, 44, 47, 49, 52, 60, 69, 80, 90, 99, 107-10, 113-4, 116, 122-3, 128, 147, 151, 154, 163-4, 182, 186, 200, 207, 213-4, 219-20, 224, 226, 230, 241-3 ,246, 250-1, 263, 274, 280, 283, 289, 290, 303, 306-7, 313, 320, 328, 330, 333, 343, 355, 358, 363, 367, 370, 372, 378-9, 382 & 397

PRESENT
(existing thoughts, feelings & experiences)

2, 9, 2, 28, 34, 37, 43, 55, 57, 59-60, 68, 74, 77, 81, 86-7, 92, 97, 102, 112, 117, 216-7 ,132, 141,143, 145-6, 150, 159, 161, 171, 173-4, 177, 197, 199, 202, 212, 218, 229, 231-2, 235, 237, 244, 257, 260, 262, 265, 279, 282, 296, 298, 305, 308, 317, 319, 326, 334, 344-5, 365, 375, 393-4, 396, 400 also pages 13, 34, 56-7 & 101

FUTURE
(goals, hopes, plans & dreams)

4, 6, 8, 22, 31, 56, 88, 100, 104, 125, 129, 148, 152, 155, 160, 166, 175, 188, 228, 236, 249, 255, 264, 278, 310 also pages 78-9 & 100

SELF-IMAGE
(teen's sense of self)

3, 10, 13, 16, 19, 25-6, 34, 41, 43, 46, 49, 51, 53, 60, 65, 69, 71, 73, 79, 86-7, 91, 97, 101-2, 106,109, 115-7, 124, 127, 133, 138, 140, 144, 148, 153, 158-9, 168, 170, 173, 179, 183, 197, 200, 215, 220, 231, 272-4, 286, 291, 310, 316, 328, 340-1, 352-3, 361, 365, 373, 379-80 also pages 12-3, 35, 56 & 100

FAMILY
(family history, development, experiences & influences)

19, 46, 54, 64, 67, 70, 78, 84-5, 100, 108, 119, 122, 125, 129, 142, 149, 152, 155-7, 166, 176, 180-1, 191, 208, 214, 221, 228, 234, 247-8, 252, 259, 268-9, 276-7, 287, 292-3, 300, 311, 313, 324, 327, 336-7, 347, 353, 355-7, 368, 376, 400 also page 57

SOCIAL
(social involvement & interaction)

SCHOOL

SPIRITUAL
(spiritual values & religious attitudes)

VALUES
(identifying, clarifying & understanding beliefs)

INTROSPECTION
(examining thoughts, feelings & motives)

THINGS TO CONSIDER

IT'S IMPORTANT TO ANSWER THE QUESTIONS.
You can answer them in any order you want. Just answer all of them eventually. If you don't think of an immediate answer, live with the question for a while. You might surprise yourself.

IF A QUESTION DOESN'T FIT, CHANGE IT.
Everybody is different. Make the questions work for you. For example, the question that asks how you feel about your siblings. What if you're an only child? So, change it to something like "This is how I feel about being an only child..."

WHAT ABOUT THE QUESTIONS YOU DON'T WANT TO ANSWER?
YOU are the author of this book. The questions in this book are about all aspects of your personality – good and bad. They may hit on areas of your life that you are not happy with or are difficult for you to think about. Remember, the important thing here is honesty – it's your book. Consider these questions a challenge and realize you may need to allow yourself time for further self-exploration.

NEED HELP?
Ask someone you're close to. Find out more about who you are by talking with those who have been part of your life. There's no telling what new stuff you'll find out!

BE CREATIVE! GET DETAILED, ADD PHOTOGRAPHS, POETRY, NEWSPAPER/MAGAZINE CLIPPINGS, WHATEVER!
This is about you, so throw in some personality. Every thing you add will increase the value of this experience. The details will increase understanding and provide greater insight into the person you are. The photos, clippings, etc. – these are the illustrations that will polish off this incredible book about YOU.

This book contains the thoughts & reflections of:

name: _____

birthdate: _____   age: _____

I began answering these questions on _____
                                            date

and completed these questions on _____
                                        date

My purpose in answering these questions is...

_____

_____

_____

my credo or philosophy

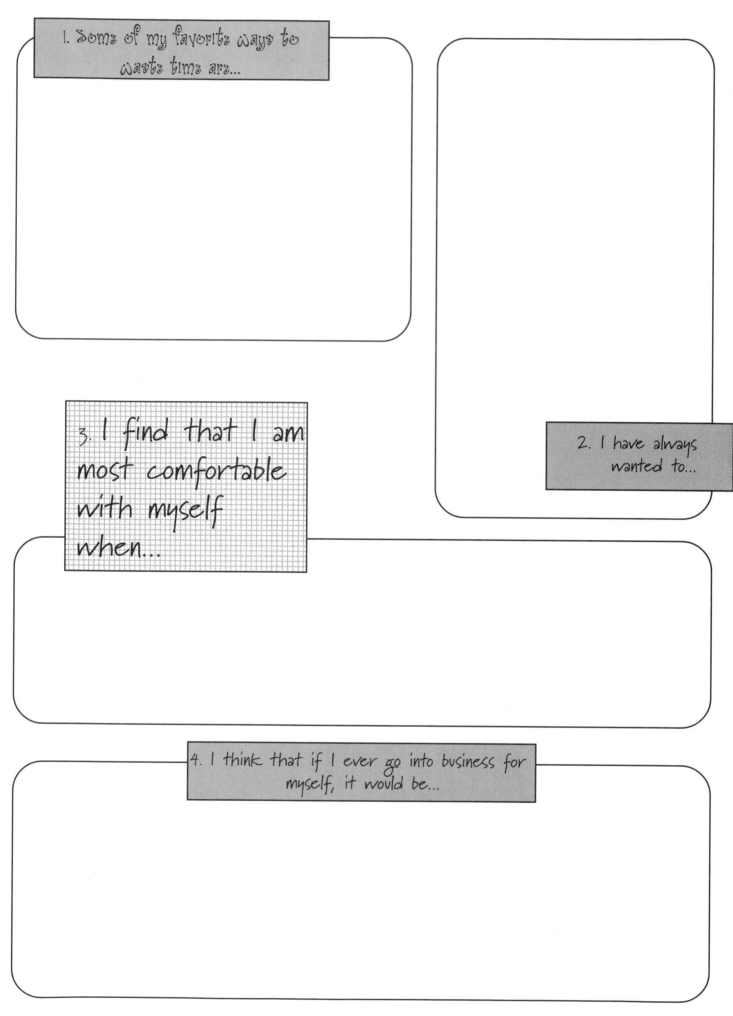

1. Some of my favorite ways to waste time are...

2. I have always wanted to...

3. I find that I am most comfortable with myself when...

4. I think that if I ever go into business for myself, it would be...

5. If I had a million dollars, I would...

6. When I think about going to college, I...

7. If I could create a holiday, it would be called...

and this is how we would celebrate it...

I'm listening for...

8. This is what I anticipate my life will be like at age 21! ...

3

9. This is how I feel about labeling people...

11. When I look at the sky I think...

10. This is how I would describe:

my physical appearance...

my personality...

12. Sometimes I feel guilty when...

4

put it in writing?

14. The 1st time I was offered marijuana or another drug was...
and this is what happened...

16. I feel really confident about myself

when it comes to...

15. I would like to change my name to....

because...

17. If I had three wishes...

18. This is how I feel about lying...

_____

_____

_____

_____

_____

19. Things my parents never told me,

but I would really like to hear...

20. If I could live one day of my life over because it was so INCREDIBLE, I would pick....

because...

6

21. Before a big test at school, I...

_____

_____

_____

_____

22. If I had to join the military today, I think I'd join the...
    because...

_____

_____

_____

_____

23. If I could trade places with someone over the age of 20, it would have to be...

I wonder.....

24. If I could change sexes for a day, I would...

25.
i am
a 'follower'
rather than a
'LEADER'
when...

26. Something
that makes me feel
REALLY stupid is...

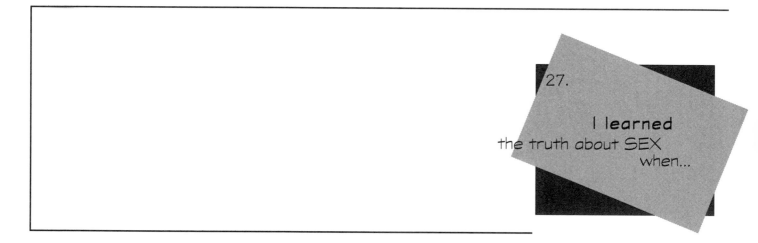

27.

I learned
the truth about SEX
when...

28. This is how
my dreams INFLUENCE my life...

30. this is **how** I feel **about** homosexuality...

29.
MY
definition of a **flirt** is...

31.
When I graduate from highschool
I want to...

32. These are **my** thoughts
on angels
& other spirits...

33. If I could get a law passed, it would be...

34. My
very best
friend
is...

because...

I see something...

35.
People
my
parent's
age
make
me
feel...

beacuse...

36. my description of a really good
leader is...

10

37. This is a list of my problems for today...

today's date is...

39. The oldest person I have known was...

and these are some things I learned about them...

38. These are my thoughts about Suicide...

40. My ideal date would include...   who? & what?

If my life was a MOVIE, this is who would be in the credits & what their job was...

Starring?

Co-starring?

Directors?

Cast?

Crew?

Producer?

Script?

Music?

Catering by

12

1O: things that make me happy are→

10 things that make me mad are >

< əɹɐ pɐs əɯ əʞɐɯ ʇɐɥʇ sƃuᴉɥʇ OԀ

< 10 things that make me sad are >

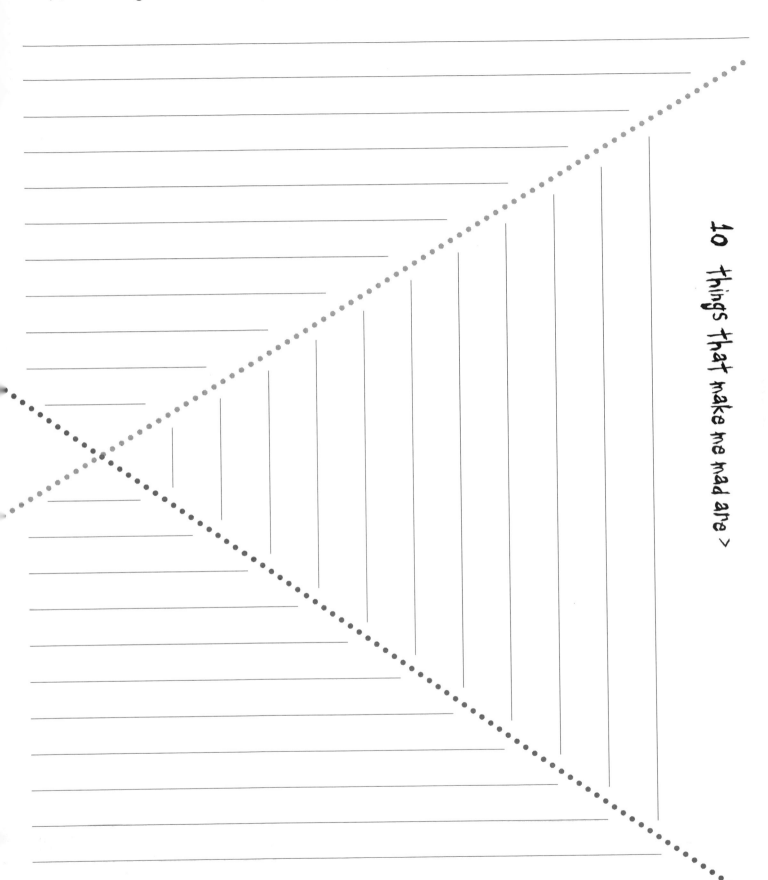

13

41. I always think it's funny when...

42. My favorite books so far are...   because...

43. MY most valued possessions are...
because...

44. In school, mY worst class ever (so far) is...
because...

45. As for the possibility of life on other planets, I tend to think...

46. A description of my perfect mate...

47. My best memories of school include...

I'm looking for...

48. Someone I would really like to spend time with & learn from is...

15

49. I was so jealous when...

51. Some songs that really fit my personality are...

50. If I owned a television station I would...

52. When I got angry as a child, I...

53. I believe that one of my gifts is...

in real life...

54. My thoughts about parents who divorce are...

55. This is what I do to get ready for a first date...

i wonder...

56. when i think of my future,

17

57. I think I might be addicted to...

58. For exercise, I like to...

_____

_____

_____

_____

_____

59. Some things that get me into trouble these days are...

60. Some habits i would really like to break...

...habits I have been able to break...

61. My definition of success is...

_____

_____

_____

62. This is what I would say to a friend who was thinking about taking drugs...

_____

_____

_____

63. These are some of my ideas on how to take care of the homeless...

I hope.....

64. I have been raised to believe in...

65. IF i found out the person i was dating was lying to ME, I would...

66. when people around me get sick, i...

67. This is what my family does for birthdays...

68. This is what I think about birth control...

70. This is what I would like to say to my father.

69. One of the most encouraging things a teacher ever said or did to me was...

71. People seem to like me because...

72. If I knew I had one week to live, I...

73. I do/do not consider myself a gossip because...

my advice is...

75.
Hospitals
make me
feel...

because...

74. my favorite things to do on a rainy day are...

76. **My favorite kind of entertainment is...**

77. When I get stressed over a test I want to make a good grade on, I...

79. The 1st time I found out a friend/acquaintance my age got pregnant i felt...

78. My description of the perfect parent is...

80. Smells that I connect with home are...

81. My dreams are usually about...

83. The perfect education would include...

82. I get confused when...

84. If someone I loved was dying, this is what I think I would do...

85. The family member that has impacted my life the most is... because...

86. I get really angry when...

87. These are some boundaries I try to set in my relation-ships...

I love to...

88. These are my thoughts on living together before marriage...

89. This is what I think about body piercing & permanent body tatoos...

90. One of the scariest places I have ever been is...

91. These are some things I do "just for myself"...

92. When I want to know what is happening in the world, I...

make a statement without saying a word...

94. If I could change just one event in history, it would be...
because...

95. This is what I would say to a friend who was considering smoking...

96. An animal I would like to come face to face with is... because...

27

97. This is what I think of myself today...

98. I avoid...

_____

_____

_____

_____

_____

99. This is a description of my worst teacher ever...

100. These are some good things my parents are doing, that I will want to do when I am a parent...

101. This is a list of people who depend on me...

_____

_____

_____

_____

102. I deal with people who are verbally or physically abusive to me by...

_____

_____

_____

_____

103. These are my thoughts about sexually transmitted diseases, including what I think of people who have them, my own personal experience with them & how I think they could best be prevented...

I believe in...

104. This is where & how I want to die...

105.
I think it's
hard
to
believe...

106. when I do GOOD
THINGS
& it goes **unnoticed,**
I feel...

107. My favorite trip
or vacation
was...

108. THE stupidest rules that
I've had to **abide by** while growing up have been...

110. as a child, the house I lived in...

109. SOME of the best ideas I ever had...

111. I would like to be on the front cover of this magazine...
the story inside would say...

112. I do/do not like to BABYSIT because...

113. The 1st time I was offered a cigarette. I...

I promise...

115. This is how I cope when my life feels out of control...

114. My first experience with death was...
& this is what I learned...

116. The cruelest thing I ever did was...

117. I feel good about myself right this minute because...

119. Some of my 1st memories of my grand-parents are...

118. If I had a million dollars to give away...

120. I think the worst way to break up with someone is...

This is a rough floor plan or sketch of the place I am living now...

These are the greatest accomplishments of my life so far...
& this is how they make me feel...

121. This is what I like to do when I am all alone...

123. When I was a child I would pretend...

122. I was raised to deal with physical pain by...

124. I would like to hold the world's record in...

125. These are my thoughts on ever having children...

126. I enjoy stories about...

127. This is how I would describe my "secret self", the self that I am afraid to show the world...

I just have to...

128. This is a description of my all time favorite teacher...

129. Some things my parents did that I am going to do differently are...

130. This is a list of friends who have died & what impact they had on me...

131. Some people think my sense of humor is...

132. Some things that I do in a typical day are...

133. This is how I handle anger...

134. A time when I've been able to sense what was going to happen before it happened was...
& it made me feel...

it would be...

135. If I could fix one physical problem of mine

like to donate my organs to others because...

136. when i die i would/would not

137. Some of my most sincere prayers & wishes...

138. I don't trust...

_____

_____

_____

_____

_____

139. These are the positive things I would want to remind myself of if I was ever to consider suicide...

140. These are the nationalities that I know are part of my heritage... & this is how I feel about that...

40

141. Some advice I would like to give to teachers is...

_____

_____

_____

_____

142. If I could take my family any place I wanted for vacation, I would...

_____

_____

_____

_____

143. If I found out today that I was pregnant or had made someone pregnant, I would...

I feel...

144. These are the qualities I look for in a friend...

145. I get along better with **boys**/girls ... because...

146. one PERSON in the **world** who knows the 'r e a l' ME is...

147. The **worst** pain I ever saw someone else in was...

it made me feel...

148. If I ever have the **opportunity** to design my own **house,** it will include...

150. my goals for **today** are...

149. These are my **thoughts** on spending my entire lifetime married to just one person...

151. a time in my **life** when I really could have used **some** psychological help or counseling was...

152. These are **my** thoughts on ever **adopting** a child...

153. When I look in the mirror & see my reflection. I...

on second thought...

155. This is what i hope my family will be like some day...

154. AS a child. my favorite hiding places were... I would go there when...

156. When i want to hide something from my family & friends, i...

157. This is how I would describe the atmosphere in my home...

159. When other people judge me by the way i look i feel...

158. The nicest compliment I ever received was...

160. If I have a child I would like to name him/her... because...

45

161. My favorite kind of music is... because...

162. These are some things I like to think about as I go to sleep...

163. When I was a kid, I thought my life at this age would be...

164. A really scary thing that happened to me was...

46

165. I would honestly be willing to give up all my possessions for... because...

166. When I am a parent, this is how I will discipline my children...

167. In my opinion, these are some things that can ruin a person's reputation...

I've always wanted...

168. These are my views on premarital sex...

47

169. Steps I have taken to make sure that my greatest fears do not happen...

170. I would have to say that my mood is usually...
because...

171. Of the sports I have participated in, my favorites are...
because...

172. At this point in my life I could write a book about...

can you imagine!

174. If my house was on fire these are the things I would try to save...

I would like to study...
　　　　　　　　because...

175. If I decide to go to college, I think that

176. the most encouraging thing anyone

in my family has ever said or done to me was...

177. My spiritual beliefs are...

178. when other people cry, I ...

_____

_____

_____

_____

_____

179. These are some lies people have told about me & how I dealt with them...

180. This is how I feel about my siblings...or...This is how I feel about being an only child...

181. This is what my parents taught me about drinking alcohol...

_____

_____

_____

_____

182. The worst punishment I ever received at school was...

_____

_____

_____

183. My experience with eating disorders such as bulimia or anorexia has been...

I promise myself...

184. My favorite season of the year is...   because...

185. the color that **best** describes ME is...

because...

186. a MEMORY I would like to be able to **erase** is...

187. My **definition** of **contentment** is...

188. These are **some** things that scare ME about becoming an **adult**...

190. i think the ideal WEDDING would include...

189. An older person I am close to is... because...

191. This is what my parents said when they first talked to me about drugs... this is what I wish they had said...

192. I want to learn more about...

193. You have my undivided attention when...

195. This is what I would say to a friend who was thinking about an abortion...

wish I may, wish I might...

194. If I could choose any animal for a pet. it would be...

because...

196. Sometimes, I just have to...

54

197. At this point in my life, I am really bad about...   because...

198. I hope I never have to...

because...

199. This is what someone might learn about me from my appearance...

200. It took real courage for me to...

Things I like about myself...

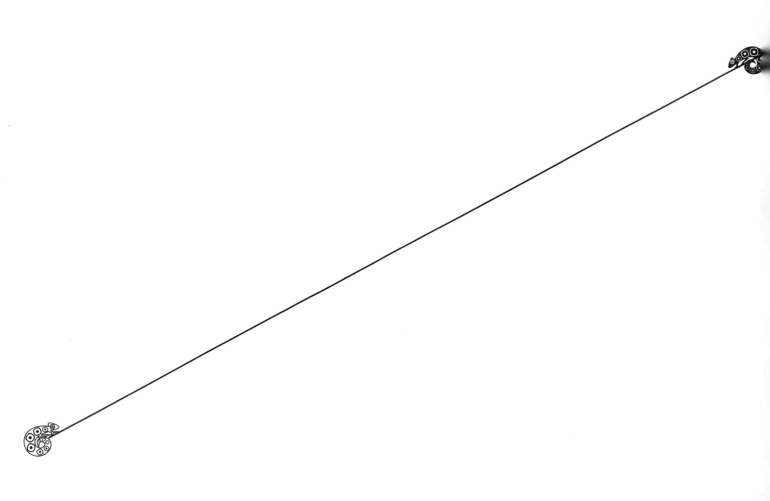

...Things about myself I'd like to change...

These are the people who I know I can trust with my life
& how they earned my trust...

201. When I am feeling depressed, I...

202. My favorite "junk" foods are ...

203. I find myself being influenced by...

204. I find myself getting confused by religion when...

205. When I give someone a gift it makes me feel...

206. these are the positive effects peer pressure has had on me...

207. My all time favorite class in school was...

because...

I think...

208. Some things I have always wanted to say to my parents, but haven't...

209. A person under the age of 50 that I would like to trade places with is... because...

210. I wonder about the existence of God or a Higher Power when...

211. If I could have 1 day all to myself & do anything I wanted, I would...

212. Sometimes, I get too preoccupied with...

213. The first time I ever had to speak in front of a group, I...

214. The worst circumstances I have had to live in were...

215. I really surprised myself when...

216. My worst headaches happen when...

217. I find myself feeling trapped when...

218. Lately, I have been day dreaming about...

_____

_____

_____

_____

_____

219. If I could apologize today for something I did a long time ago, it would have to be...

220. One of the most destructive things a teacher ever said or did to me was...

221. When my parents get angry with each other, they...

_____

_____

_____

_____

222. Of all my friends, the one most likely to make something of him/
herself is...   because...

_____

_____

_____

_____

223. This is how I tend to respond to authority figures...

Life is...

224. The 1st book I can recall having read to me was...

225. my greatest FEARS in life are... because...

226. my NEEDS at this moment are...

227. My parents' attitude toward life seems to be...

228. When I die, this is what I'd like for my family & friends to do...

230. one special moment that stands **OUT** in my mind is...

229. My thoughts on **divorce** are...

231. These are some **things** I **choose** to say 'no' to...

232. Some of my favorite things **to do** with my **friends** are...

233. Some really rotten things I have done are...

I believe in...

235.
School would be more useful and interesting to me if...

234. These are some memories about my father...

236. By the time I am 40, I hope my life will be...

237. When I am uptight & stressed out, this is how I deal with it...

239. The person or event having the greatest impact on me spiritually is...

238. If I could live one year of my life over again...

240. Some of my favorite poetry is...   because...

241. The best gift I have received is...

242. When I was a kid I wanted to grow up to be...

243. My wants at this moment are...

244. The style of music that best fits my life right now is...   because...

245. This is what I would die for...

246. my worst memories of school include...

247. Some-times the only way I can get attention from my parents is...

love is...

248. This is how I would describe my father's personality...

249. When I am 30, I will be...

250. A time when I thought I was 'losing my mind' was...

251. Some of the biggest mistakes I ever made were...

252. This is what I learned from watching my parent's relationship...

253. When I want to break up with someone, I think the best way to do it is...

because...

254. Thinking of these people always brings a smile to my face...

255. Things that concern me about the future include...

256. These are the political issues I feel most passionate about...

257. This is what I think about pornography...

258. Sometimes I wonder...

_____

_____

_____

_____

_____

259. This is how I would describe my mother's personality...

260. This is a list of bones that I have broken and/or scars I have and how they happened....

261. If the story of my life was made into a novel, the title would be... because...

_____

_____

_____

262. This is who the author (coauthors) of the current chapter of my life are...

_____

_____

_____

263. These are some of the names of the chapters of my life so far...

I lean toward...

264. These are some possible names for future chapters of my life...

265. sometimes I have dreams or nightmares about...

266. MY favorite work of art is...

267. Communicating with older people is... because...

268. This is how money affects my family...

269. this is how I would describe my siblings...

270. the perfect life would include.

271. My religious heritage includes... & this is how I feel about that...

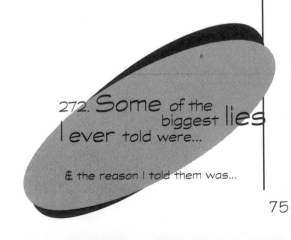

272. Some of the biggest lies I ever told were...

& the reason I told them was...

273. I disappointed myself when...

274. I feel I was abused or taken advantage of as a child when...

I want to know...

275. I'm not a very good cook when it comes to...

276. Some of our family traditions or rituals include...

277. This is how I am like my mother...

279. My thoughts on the importance of popularity & people who put popularity above almost everything else are...

278. My dream career would be to...

280. A really great advertisement is...

Ten things I hope to accomplish in my lifetime are...

1

2

3

4

5

6

7

8

9

10

Ten places I hope to visit in my lifetime are...

1

2

3

4

5

6

7

8

9

10

These are my predictions of what the world will be like in 50 years....

281. I think all children should have...

282. Some fears I have about dating are...

283. As a child, these are some things I did on rainy days...

284. Some of my own personal habits that people may find a little strange...

285. Things in nature that have special meaning to me are... because...

286. When confronted with difficulty or a challenge, I...

287. Some of the family secrets that nobody ever talks about are...

how will I know...

288. These are the religions I would like to know more about... because...

289. A memory I would like to be able to frame and hang on my wall is...

290. Some unlikely people I can remember having a 'crush' on...

291. Sometimes I have problems making friends because...

292. The fairy tale characters my parents most remind me of are...

because...

293. My parents' general attitude toward me seems to be...

294. If it was possible to program my dreams, tonight I would like to dream about...

295. What are some things that you will not tolerate...

296. Some of my favorite musical groups are... because...

297. My definition of the word 'miracle' is...

298. My passions are...

_____

_____

_____

my poisons are...

_____

_____

_____

299. This is what I would say or do to a friend who was considering suicide...

300. The most destructive thing anyone in my family has ever said or done to me was...

84

301. When people cheat in school and get away with it I...

_____

_____

_____

_____

302. A time when I was unfaithful to someone I cared about was... and this was the result...

_____

_____

_____

303. One of the most embarrassing things that ever happened to me was...

I'll never...

304. MY favorite holiday is...   because...

305. my favorite TV shows are...

because...

306. these are some of the most rebelious things I have ever done...

307. The sickest I ever felt was...

308. My definition of discrimination is...

310. this is **w**here & how
I hope
to live...

309. I find
myself **f e e l i n g**
lazy when...

311. The worst **punishment** I
ever received at **home** was...

312. MY thoughts
about
MONEY
are...

313. The best family vacation we ever had...

315. The role of spirituality in my life today is...

I imagine...

314. Some of my favorite smells are...

because...

316. I tend to be a 'leader' rather than a 'follower' when...

317. These are things I find healing or soothing...

319. This is how I feel about small groups of people who don't accept others...

318. This is how I feel about Politics & politicians...

320. The greatest heartache in my life came when...

321. I am curious about...

322. To me, one of life's greatest mysteries is...

323. Times in my life when I have felt all alone were...

324. Family members who I consider to have addiction problems are...

325. Being around people who are my grandparent's age makes me feel... because...

326. these are my concerns about our planet...

327. When it comes to the subject of dating, my parents seem to feel...

sometimes...

328. I wonder how my life would have turned out differently if...

91

329. Increasingly, juveniles are being tried as adults for crimes such as rape or murder. These are my thoughts on the issue and why I think this way...

330. I think some of the most beautiful sights I have ever seen are...

331. I think a person is 'old' when... because...

332. This is list of teams, clubs & other organizations that I have been a part of & some thoughts about that...

333. If I could live one day of my life over & change something that made it a terrible day, I would pick...   because...

334. These are some things I always find myself putting off until tomorrow...

335. These are some things that always seem to make me cry...

336. This is what I would like to say to my mother...

93

337. This is how I am like my father...

338. My favorite day of the week is...
because...

_____

_____

My favorite time of day is... because...

_____

_____

339. If I could live anywhere in the world for the remainder of my life, it would be... because...

340. These are the feelings that are the hardest for me to express... & this is how I deal with them...

94

341. When an emergency situation develops, I...

_____

_____

_____

342. The most inspirational thing that has ever happened to me was...

_____

_____

_____

343. One secret I have held on to for years & never told anybody is...

I'll always...

344. My favorite spectator sports are...   because...

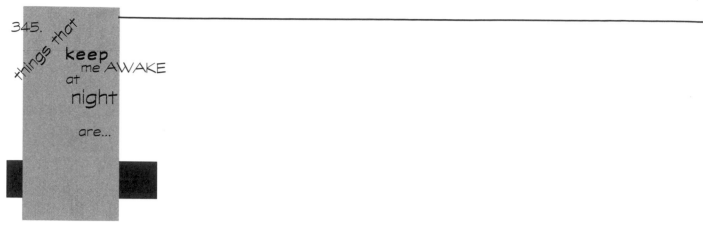

345. things that **keep** me AWAKE at night are...

346. my favorite fairy tale is... because...

347. When my **parents** are angry with me, they...

348. The **people** I am most comfortable around are... because...

350. this is what I think a good movie should include...

349. MY thoughts on marriage are...

351. These are my thoughts on Darwin's THEORY of Evolution...

352. Some things I would be good at teaching others are... because...

353. I am embarrassed by... because...

let's pretend...

355. As a child, these were some of the things that got me into trouble the most...

354. My idea of the perfect community is...

356. The worst time I ever experienced with my parents or other relatives was when...

357. The most controlling person in my life is...

359. I think sports should/should not be a priority in my school because...

358. These are some memories about my very first romance...

360. I find it hard to get along with this type of person... because...

Ten pieces of advice I would like to pass on to myself
to read in the future are.........

1.

2.

3.

4.

5.

6.

7.

8.

9.

10.

Just in case I die today, I am leaving these messages for the following people...

361. I suffered a complete loss of confidence when...

362. A time I put myself at risk to help others was...

363. My most memorable encounter with a police officer was...

364. These are the words I would like to find in my fortune cookie...

365. These are things I do to make other people happy...

366. these are my thoughts on having plastic surgery...

367. Some things I have done that I really regret are...

If only I...

368. Some memories of my mother include...

369. The first time a friend/acquaintance my age had sex was...
and this is how I felt when I heard about it...

370. These are people who have influenced me to do things I thought were wrong...
& this is how they convinced me...

371. The most difficult decision I have had to make recently is...

372. Going back as far as I can remember, my first best friend was...

...some of the things we used to do together were...

373. These are some things I do to get the attention of a person who I would like to date...

374. I believe that the greatest world leader of all time was....

because...

375. These are my thoughts about 'assisted' suicide...

376. this is what my parents said when they first talked to me about smoking...

377. This is what I think life after death is going to be like...

378. When I was a child, I enjoyed collecting...

_____

_____

the things I like to collect now...

_____

_____

379. My thoughts about dieting & my personal experience, if any, are...

380. If I found out the person I was dating was abusing (or addicted to) drugs or alcohol, I would...

381. These are my thoughts on religion in general...

_____

_____

_____

_____

382. My first friend/acquaintance that died a violent death was...

& this is how I felt...

_____

_____

_____

_____

383. These are my thoughts on having to pay taxes on the money I earn...

I can.....

384. When I think of these things it always makes me smile...

385. these are my thoughts on cloning human beings...

386. these are some things I have done to help someone in need.,,

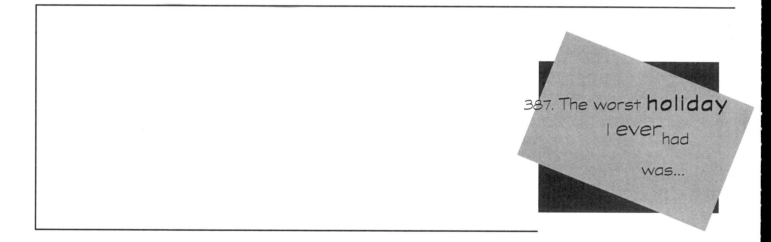

387. The worst holiday I ever had was...

388. MY definition of a "soul mate" is...   ...these people fit that definition for me...

389. This is how I **feel** about using or having to listen to foul language...

390. when I find out **someone** I know is HIV positive or has AIDS, I...

391. my favorite comic book or animated character is... because......

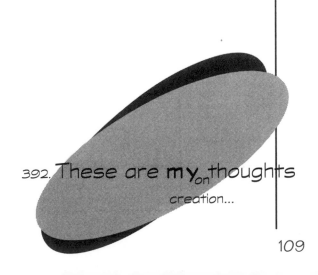

392. These are **my** thoughts on creation...

393. This is how I feel about abortion...

395. To maintain a loving relationship over a long period of time i think these things must happen...

can you believe...

394. This is how I feel about mixing school & work...

396. my idea of a party includes...

397. the time in my life that i cried the hardest was...

399. The movie i've watched the most times is... because...

How many times?

398. Writing in this book has...

400. If I could change something about my family. it would be...

say what?

a picture is worth a thousand words??

Things I am grateful for...

Just thinking about all of my possibilities...